MAZECRAFT
MAZE GAMES AND COOL PUZZLES

SCHOLASTIC

YOU CAN FIND SOLUTIONS TO ALL THE PUZZLES ON PAGES 30 TO 32.

This edition created in 2018 by
Arcturus Publishing Limited 26/27 Bickels Yard,
151–153 Bermondsey Street, London SE1 3HA
Copyright © Arcturus Holdings Limited

ISBN 978-1-78828-290-1

10 9 8 7 6 5 4 3 2 1   15 16 17 18 19

Printed in China

CH006057NT
Supplier 29, Date 0118, Print run 7122

Packaged for Arcturus by Infinite Jest Ltd
Text: Katherine Sully
Illustration: Peter Lawson
Design: Jessica Moon and Linda Storey
Maze Design: Simon Ward
Project Management: Gill Shepherd

Editor for Arcturus: Joe Harris
Cover Illustration: Adam Clay

HOW TO USE THIS BOOK

Hi there! I'm Ace McDanger,
world-famous treasure hunter,
and I'm looking for an intrepid assistant.
Are you brave enough to act as my guide?

MOON BASE

Space aliens have invaded the moon base!
Sneak past them to reach the treasure,
but don't step on a bomb!

Collect all four precious jewels along the way and check them off.

SHOW ME A SAFE PATH TO THE TREASURE CHEST.

THE CREATURES IN EACH MAZE BLOCK THE ROUTE.

LOOK OUT FOR THE TERRIBLE TRAPS!

GATHER ALL THE JEWELS.

WICKED WEBS

Creep past these cave spiders and their webs to reach the treasure without being caught!

Collect all four precious jewels along the way and check them off.

MARS MAZE

These Martians don't look friendly! Steer clear of the creatures and avoid falling down any craters. Can you reach the treasure?

Collect all four precious jewels along the way and check them off.

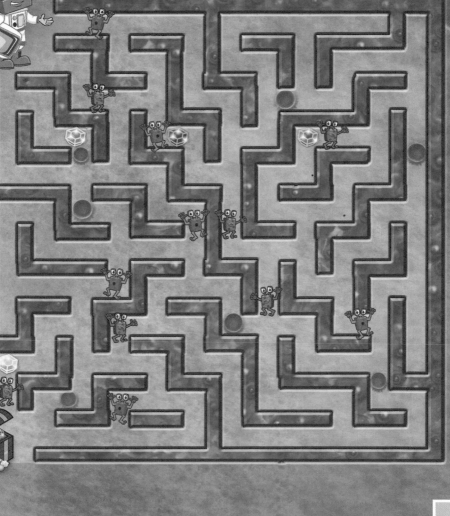

WHERE, WOLF?

This forest is packed full of dangerous traps... and a hungry werewolf! Can you find a safe path to the treasure?

Collect all four precious jewels along the way and check them off.

ALIEN INVASION

Don't let the aliens spot you! Find the lever to switch off the force field around the treasure.

Collect all four precious jewels along the way and check them off.

WOLF TRAILS

Which path should Ace follow?
One trail leads straight to the treasure,
but the other two lead to hungry wolves!

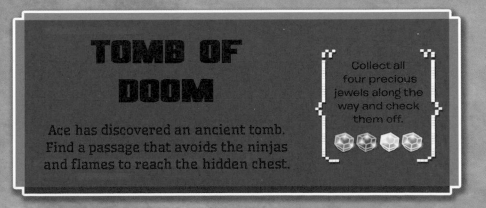

TOMB OF DOOM

Ace has discovered an ancient tomb. Find a passage that avoids the ninjas and flames to reach the hidden chest.

Collect all four precious jewels along the way and check them off.

DEADLY DIVE

Steer clear of stinging tentacles and prickly pink coral as you dive down to search for the lost treasure.

Collect all four precious jewels along the way and check them off.

GREEDY WEEDS

Hack your way through this overgrown maze to discover the treasure chest. Avoid the man-eating jungle plants!

Collect all four precious jewels along the way and check them off.

ZOMBIE ZONE

You'll need to be brave to get past these horrible zombies and fires. The treasure is hidden in the basement.

Collect all four precious jewels along the way and check them off.

BLACK LAGOON

Beware of the monsters in the Black Lagoon! They will try to grab you on your way to find the treasure chest.

Collect all four precious jewels along the way and check them off.

MET A YETI?

Your next quest is to free the treasure from the frozen ice. But watch out for the yetis!

Collect all four precious jewels along the way and check them off.

A B C

CREEPY CREEPERS

One of these tangled vines leads to a treasure chest, but the other two lead to man-eating plants! Choose carefully...

TAIL STING

Beware of stinging scorpions and prickly cacti as you cross the desert to claim the chest.

Collect all four precious jewels along the way and check them off.

FAIRY FOREST

This forest is filled with magic and spells. If you bump into a pixie, fairy, or goblin, they will send you back to the start!

Collect all four precious jewels along the way and check them off.

BACK IN TIME

A volcanic blast has transported you back to the time of the dinosaurs! Find and circle the twelve hidden words in the grid below.

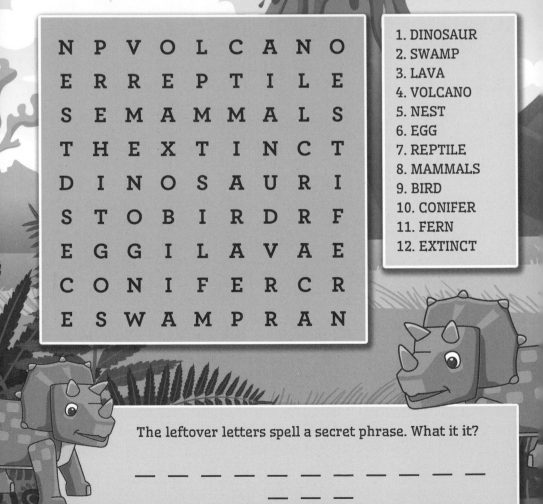

```
N P V O L C A N O
E R R E P T I L E
S E M A M M A L S
T H E X T I N C T
D I N O S A U R I
S T O B I R D R F
E G G I L A V A E
C O N I F E R C R
E S W A M P R A N
```

1. DINOSAUR
2. SWAMP
3. LAVA
4. VOLCANO
5. NEST
6. EGG
7. REPTILE
8. MAMMALS
9. BIRD
10. CONIFER
11. FERN
12. EXTINCT

The leftover letters spell a secret phrase. What it it?

_ _ _ _ _ _ _ _ _ _ _ _

_ _ _

HIPPO SWAMP

Tread carefully through the swamp, avoiding the mantraps and hippos. There's treasure to be found!

Collect all four precious jewels along the way and check them off.

ERUPTION!

Find the treasure before the volcano erupts! Beware of dinosaurs living deep below the surface.

Collect all four precious jewels along the way and check them off.

ICE QUEEN

This chilly castle is home to ice monsters and polar bears. Find a safe route to the treasure and escape the Ice Queen!

Collect all four precious jewels along the way and check them off.

MOON BASE

Space aliens have invaded the moon base! Sneak past them to reach the treasure, but don't step on a bomb!

Collect all four precious jewels along the way and check them off.

DINO PARK

Somewhere in this prehistoric park is a hidden treasure chest. Can you reach it before feeding time?

Collect all four precious jewels along the way and check them off.

WILD WOOD

You've spotted more treasure in the wild wood. Can you get past the Bigfeet, piranhas, and traps to reach it?

Collect all four precious jewels along the way and check them off.

ICE PUZZLE

Can you follow the right path to rescue the frozen penguin? Be careful... the other paths lead to hungry polar bears!

VILE VIKINGS

The Vikings are coming! Save the treasure before they plunder the island. Look out for traps!

Collect all four precious jewels along the way and check them off.

SHARK ATTACK

Are you getting a sinking feeling? This deep-sea treasure is guarded by sharks and prickly coral.

Collect all four precious jewels along the way and check them off.

RAT TRAP!

Massive mousetraps have been set all over this house. Avoid the rats and traps to get to the treasure.

Collect all four precious jewels along the way and check them off.

SHARK REEF

Find and circle the shark names below. The leftover letters will spell out some friendlier sea animals.

```
H A M M E R H E A D
D S A N D T I G E R
O C A R I B B E A N
N L P R E Q U I E M
U Z W H I T E T I P
R E C A T S H A R K
S B S A W S H A R K
E R B L A C K T I P
H A I N C A R P E T
W O B B E G O N G S
```

1. BLACKTIP
2. CATSHARK
3. WHITETIP
4. SANDTIGER
5. CARPET
6. REQUIEM
7. HAMMERHEAD
8. CARIBBEAN
9. WOBBEGONG
10. NURSE
11. SAWSHARK
12. ZEBRA

What word do the leftover letters spell out? Write it in the space below.

_ _ _ _ _ _ _ _

PUZZLE SOLUTIO S

Each maze has red and green lines to show different achievements.

THE RED PATH LEADS TO THE TREASURE CHEST.

THE GREEN PATHS LEAD TO THE JEWELS.

page 4

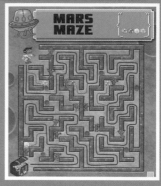

page 5

page 6

page 7

Answer: follow the red line to find the lever

page 8

page 9

page 10

page 11

page 12

page 13

page 14

page 15

Answer: B

page 16

page 17

BACK IN TIME

N P VOLCANO
E R R REPTILE
S E MAMMALS
T H EXTINCT
DINOSAUR C
I S T BIRD I F
EGG O LAVA E
CONIFER R R
E SWAMP R A N

page 18

Answer: Prehistoric Era

page 19

page 20

page 21

page 22

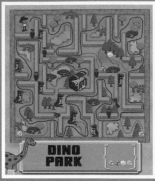
page 23

page 24

page 25

page 26

page 27

page 28

page 29
Answer: Dolphins